HURON COUNTY PUBLIC

W9-CKD-171

HURON COUNTY LIBRARY

2 008 118920 9

Date Due

Blyth -JAN/87		
MAR - 5 1987		
STHApr88		
HENApr89		
JUN 2 6 1989		
AU Jan90		

971.002
Nic

28720

NICOL, E.

THE U.S. OR US.

The US or US: What's the Difference, Eh?

Hurtig Publishers
Edmonton

28720

NOV 27 1986

Copyright © 1986 by Eric Nicol and Dave More

All rights reserved. No part of this book may be reproduced or transmitted in any form by any means, electronic, electrical, mechanical, chemical, optical, or otherwise, including photocopying and recording, or by any information storage or retrieval system, without written permission from the publisher, except for brief passages quoted by a reviewer in a newspaper or magazine.

Hurtig Publishers Ltd.
10560 – 105 Street
Edmonton, Alberta
Canada T5H 2W7

Canadian Cataloguing in Publication Data
Nicol, Eric, 1919-
  The U.S. or us

  ISBN 0-88830-296-7

  1. National characteristics, Canadian–
Anecdotes, facetiae, satire, etc.   2. National
characteristics, American–Anecdotes, facetiae,
satire, etc.   I. More, Dave.   II. Title.
FC173.N53 1986   971'.002'07   C86-091287-6
F1026.4.N53 1986

Printed and bound in Canada

For want of the poem, the Canadian book was lost.
For want of the book, CanLit was lost.
For want of CanLit, our culture was lost.
For want of a culture, our political independence was lost.
For want of political independence, our nation was lost.
For want of our nation, world peace was lost.
So for God's sake print this, or get nuked!

Publisher's Note

The opinions expressed in this book are definitely those of the authors and in no way, at no time, and under no circumstance whatsoever even remotely reflect the views of the publisher.

Furthermore, the national characters in this book are intended as caricatures; any resemblance to actual Canadians — alive, dead, or simply hibernating — is accidental.

Contents

Introduction

Why We Beg to Differ

Canadians want to preserve their cultural identity

The Rosemarie *syndrome*

2

A Canadian is defined as an American with the spark plugs removed. Conversely, an American is a Canadian who found his ID.

Citizens of the United States put a high price on their Americanism. Canadians are reduced to clear. Previously frozen.

Canada is dependent on the United States for its culture, its economy, its defence, and its baby alligators. In contrast, the only thing that the States really needs from Canada is water. Some U.S. senators believe that if a way can be found to rid Canada of its impurities (the Canadian people), the country has a tremendous potential as a reservoir.

Is this a sound basis for free trade?

That is the question being debated since Prime Minister Mulroney made it clear that his meetings with President Reagan were not just a crush but the beginning of a meaningful relationship. According to the polls of public opinion, most Canadians favour free trade with the U.S. Anything they can get for free, they'll take. But how much of this enthusiasm stems from the novelty of seeing a Canadian prime minister go the States to hug *another man*? May this not be backlash against the previous PM, Pierre Trudeau, who made no attempt to conceal his preference for women?

Your authors have analysed the options for Canada as follows:

1. Go for free trade with the U.S. (Also known as Amway Anschluss.)

Free trade means removing all duties except taking out the garbage. It is the opposite of *protectionism* (spray or roll-on). By imposing duties on imports, protectionism protects the jobs of the country's workers who are being overpaid to turn out inferior products. *I.e.*, most of our immediate family.

The problem for Canadians is that, even if free trade with the U.S. increases their income, they will use the extra money to leave the coun-

Getting the annual Canada goose

try. Canada has a frightful imbalance of tourist trade with the States. At any given moment, most of Canada's gross national product is climbing into a bus bound for Las Vegas. For free trade to work, millions more Americans must spend their winter holidays in Canada, possibly as an alternative to capital punishment.

2. Keep Canada poor but honest. Are Canadians prepared to pay the price for free trade, namely, losing their national identity, and if so how would they tell that it was gone?

"O.K., Jonesy, let's see . . . Three lifers on permanent holiday to Baffin Island . . . three sets of skis . . . nine pairs of long undies . . . sixty dozen Chapsticks . . ."

French Canada will be the first to notice that increased sales of their maple syrup are offset by the fact that the maple trees now belong to the United Fruit Company. It will take the English-speaking provinces longer to realize that they have been absorbed by the U.S. Newfoundland may never find out.

Many Canadian nationalists fear that eco-

6

nomic union with the United States will lead to political union, making the Queen redundant. And Ronald Reagan may not look all that great riding sidesaddle in a skirt.

In the pages that follow, the reader will find an objective, reasoned study of the American and Canadian lifestyles and, indeed, deathstyles. (More Canadians choose cremation — it's their last chance to get warm.) We start with religion: the Almighty Dollar.

D.M. & E.N.

Most Canadian queens are lent from Britain

Most American queens are something else

Canadian dollar accepted at par

Chapter One

Why Trade Is None of Our Business

Most American corporations view Canada as an economic colony. If these were biblical times, Pontius Pilate would have been sent by the U.S. parent company to Toronto to be head of American Chariots of Canada Ltd. When Pilate heard that a young Canadian had been born who would one day build a good Canadian chariot, he would have ordered Security to slaughter every infant with grease on his diaper.

The U.S. economic empire has been built by American companies smart enough not to march around in the colony wearing steel leg-warmers and flogging the natives to work harder. The American

13

emperor remains on Wall street, confident that sooner or later the nominal head of the vassal state will come to him, hat in hand, begging for a loan in return for the right to replace the legislature with an Exxon oil rig.

One reason why the American economic raj prevails in Canada is that American investors are prepared to take *chances*, whereas Canadians see these as *risks*. To a Canadian, an opportunity is a risk unless it is fully covered by insurance. He is insured against unemployment, death, and loss of the engagement ring. Only then does he feel free to lose his job, fall under a bus, or get married.

The Canadian is prepared to embark on the Unknown so long as it has been approved by *Consumer Reports*.

Not so the average American. To an American, not only is the cup half full rather than half empty, but Lady Luck is hovering with the coffee pot. What awaits the American is Destiny, the Canadian, Fate.

This is why Americans are avid inventors. They are great ones for discovering something new in their garage. Canadians don't expect to find anything in their garage except their car. An American car.

Can the production tables be turned?

Which side would Canada be on, in the event of nuclear war between Coke and Pepsi? Would the country try to remain neutral, by drinking prune juice?

Canadian secret service — the sap watch

Has the new Canadian spy agency, which took over from the RCMP because their spurs were clanking, been able to break the code of Colonel Sanders' secret recipe for Kentucky Fried Chicken?

Some Canadian companies have decided that the best defence is attack. They are buying up properties in cities like New York and Dallas, the equivalent of David gaining controlling interest of the private parts of Goliath. Conjecture now is: *Will Canada launch a take-over bid for the United States?* The scenario:

With the backing of Hong Kong billionaires, Canada buys enough U.S. government bonds to become a major shareholder of Uncle Sam. It then becomes a simple matter of persuading the remaining shareholders, American citizens, that the U.S. will pay better dividends if run by Ottawa. The advertising campaign stresses

- Canada will allow the States to retain the present management in Washington, as well as the flag, the Dallas Cowboys Cheerleaders, and other important institutions;
- the Canadian embassy moves to Fort Knox;
- the value of the U.S. dollar is unaffected, but Liberace's clothing allowance is broadened to include Canada's national debt;
- free corsages for the ladies.

Are Canadians too proud of their inferiority complex?

Attractive though a Canadian take-over of the U.S.A. looks on paper, it will require a certain bravura performance to convince the American shareholders that Canada can run North America better than does General Motors.

Such a performance runs counter to the Canadian inferiority complex.

What *is* the Canadian inferiority complex? On a national scale, it is the response of Groucho Marx

16

The Dr. Central and Mr. Hyde Park syndrome

when invited to join an exclusive country club: "I wouldn't join any club that would have me as a member." Some analysts have tried to convince Canadians that they do not have an inferiority complex — they really *are* inferior. But the nation refuses to be comforted. It knows that having an inferiority complex is excellent protection against the hazards of success. The qualitative guideline is: *If a Canadian has what it takes, why didn't he take it to the States?*

Most Canadians reject the idea of economic and/or political union with the States, fearing the loss of their main access to humility. To become suddenly part of a superpower would create a radical change of pressure for Canadians. They could contract the nationalist bends. Effects such as:

- smoke damage from trying to light two cigars at once;
- grief over loss of a dear one (Hockey Night in Canada);
- confusion from switching the object of hatred from Toronto to Cuba;
- combined delight and horror (the Mr. Hyde Syndrome) at being transformed into the Ugly American.

It is therefore important for a Canadian to know when he is turning into an American. If indeed it hasn't already happened.

Chapter Two

When Is an American?

Dropping the pilot (Canadian style)

The average European, Asian, or alien from outer space views Canadians as Americans because they inhabit North America. Yet Mexicans too are North Americans, and nobody calls *them* Americans unless he wants a taco shoved up his nose. What shapes the Canadian character to fit into the blender?

Canadians who wish to be distinguished from Americans have asked that citizens of the neighbouring republic (the U.S.A.) be called Usasians. Or Statics. Neither name has caught on. It is said that you can always tell an Englishman, though you can't tell him much. In contrast, you can't tell a Canadian, though he's dying to hear.

Canadians don't help matters, the way they tell themselves. The francophones refer to two-thirds of the population as *les maudits Anglais*, while the anglophone resents "the French" for trying to shove their tongue down his throat (a French kiss).

Thus "American" means the highest common factor, "Canadian" the lowest common denominator. The world regards the States to be a whole that is greater than the sum of its parts. Canada doesn't add up.

Luckily, history is to blame

The superior cohesiveness of Americans results from the fact that immigrants to the U.S. left the old country of their own accord, whereas immigrants to Canada were sent there, by relatives who needed their room to store vegetables.

The Pilgrim Fathers were Quakers feeling their oats. A spirited group of émigrés, they were ready to talk turkey with the Indians and replace tobacco by lighting up a witch. But very few of the early settlers to Canada considered themselves to be pilgrims. If Canada was the promised land, they soon learned the difference between land promised by God and by the CPR.

Canadians still might have achieved a sense of unity if they had enjoyed the advantage of a bloody revolution, in order to achieve their independence. The best that Canada could manage was a couple of

Little Louis Riel and his dad's aspen tree

minor rebellions, led by men who were either crazy or members of parliament, or both. Louis Riel, though he has made a comeback in recent years as a national hero, never caught on like George Washington because he lost much of his impact after he was hanged. Also Canada had no charming little story about young Louis chopping down his father's cherry tree and later admitting that the axe was to blame.

George Washington is revered in the U.S. because he was a soldier who fought against the English. John A. Macdonald killed a lot of Scotch, but only as a civilian.

Nor has Canada had a great civil war, to create an emotional bond as well as Confederate money. In Canada, brother has never had to fight against brother, unless they were drafted by different hockey teams. A Canadian novel about the struggle between the North and the South would be titled *Gone with the Whiff*.

In terms of civil strife, the closest that Canada has come to the Burning of Atlanta has been René Lévesque smoking three packs a day.

Les Québecois waited too long to put the mayor of Montreal in a Renault and have him ride through the province shouting "The British are coming! The British are coming!" The British were already there. All the French could do was change the street signs into French and go back to bed.

The only war that Canada has fought on its own territory (the War of 1812) was against the Americans. Apparently 1812 was not a good year for wars. Nobody said anything memorable. The British troops sacked Washington, but they were professionals and referred all requests for interviews to their agent in London.

Are there enough United Empire Loyalists left in Canada to resist union with the States? To give their lives, if necessary? Not if it jeopardizes their American Express card.

Winning the West

The mystique of the Old West strengthens Americanism, while Canada's West has suffered from an excess of law and order. American Indians take satisfaction from Custer's Last Stand, while Canadian Indians are stuck with a bunch of Brand-X massacres. (Although this situation may yet be rectified,

The American West was settled in relative peace

The settling of the Canadian West was a period of great
upheavals and unrest

it's not the same — scalping hundreds of government lawyers.)

The person who ruined Canada's Old West was Queen Victoria. She had a dampening effect on the rule of the gun, not carrying a six-shooter herself and rarely bellying up to the bar of a saloon.

While Americans developed their hallowed tradition of violence, thanks to the uninhibited gun-

American

Canadian

American

Canadian

slinging of the Earps and other explosions, in Canada the main-street shootout never flourished, as an art form. The Mountie insisted not only on staying on his horse but explaining the Queen's law. This discouraged the quick-draw artist, who had to go to the States to make a living. In the Canadian High Noon, the Newfie draws a half-hour later.

To this day, every American citizen considers it his sacred right to carry a handgun. His holiday in Canada starts badly when Canadian Customs require him to check his Smith & Wesson pistol at the border. Fortunately for Canada's tourist trade, Americans are permitted to bring in hunting rifles. The Canadian philosophy is that the larger the weapon, the less dangerous it is. An American M-1 tank can enter Canada without having to declare a thing.

In contrast, the Canadian travelling into the United States may be frisked for fruit flies. The Americans are not concerned about guns, but woe betide the visitor caught carrying an unregistered grape.

Ethnic volatility

Another factor making Americans different from the decent dullness of Canadians is the ethnic mix. The States have been described as a melting pot, the various races being homogenized by the heat of patriotism. Canada, however, is a tossed salad. Whose French dressing needs something.

The American melting pot

The Canadian salad bowl

This criticism fails to recognize that the American character has enjoyed an enormous advantage, in terms of being animated, because of the massive infusion of blacks. The blacks have contributed:

(a) soul music, soul food and the soul handshake;
(b) football players, the Harlem Globetrotters and Gary Coleman;

The old New Brunswick customs of "high-mitting" and "toque-breaking"

(c) a new English vulgate (Hashlish), Greek and Latin being replaced by derivatives of the poppy.

Because Canada received relatively few black slaves, for Canadians

(a) grey is beautiful;
(b) rhythm is a Catholic contraceptive;
(c) athletic supremacy (hockey, curling) ends if the ice melts;
(d) a mixed marriage means a man and a woman.

In recent years, large numbers of Italians have settled in and around Toronto, diversifying the city's traditional garment industry: stuffing shirts. While this ethnic injection has helped to make Canada's commercial capital more aware of food as one of the pleasures of life, the Italian community has itself been modified by the vast emotional inertia of the incumbents. Evidence:

1. When the Canadian Mafia puts out a contract, this has to be signed by two witnesses. The Kiss of Death is on the nose.
2. In Canada, the opera audience still does not lustily boo a bad performance. The best it can manage is a sitting ovation.
3. Canadian Italians have no patron saint equivalent to St. Francis of Sinatra.

Apparently what the Canadian sees in the mirror is not just an American who has had a bad night.

It follows that symbiosis of the two peoples is too complex a phenomenon to be dismissed without examination of the survival rate of the African bird that finds its food amid the teeth of the crocodile. How conscientious is Uncle Sam about flossing? Is the Canada goose fast enough on its feet?

Hazards of being a kid

In America it is difficult to eat ice cream

Hazards of being a kid

In Canada it is difficult to eat ice cream

Tasty-looking frost on metal fences

Saturday night baths

The icebreaker incident

Chapter Three

Self-Government
& Other Fantasies

Canadians know more about the American system of government than Americans know about the Canadian system of government, because the Speech from the Throne gets less play than Johnny Carson's monologue. Carson has better writers, and he knows something that the governor general doesn't: it's harder to be a sit-down comedian.

The American perception of Canadian government goes something like this:

The Queen comes to govern Canada on weekends when England is too warm for horse racing. She stays at the Royal York in Toronto and issues enough orders to keep Canada going till the Duke of Edinburgh can fly over between polo matches. A nature-lover, the Duke keeps the Canadians honest about turning over half the furs they cheat from the Indians.

The Queen's permanent representative in Canada is the viceroy, who had to leave India when they took away his elephant. The duties of the viceroy:

(a) Keep the throne polished.
(b) Check the royal carriage for salt corrosion.
(c) Inspect the bearskin hat that Canada supplies to British guardsmen, making sure that the bear is not still in it.
(d) Wear a funny cocked hat on state occasions such as a Canadian production of Gilbert and Sullivan's *H.M.S. Pinafore*.

Canada unfortunately elects socialists to parliament, despite distribution of CIA manuals on how to deal with unfriendly terrorists.

The Reds occupy the House of Communists (or Lower Canada). They are kept in line by the MPs, whose sergeant-at-arms clouts them with an enormous mace if they try to seize power.

The people's representatives who believe in God and free enterprise are found in the Senate (Upper Canada), which is like the American Senate except for the absence of life.

Together, the two Canadian houses are called *parliament*, because the buildings look like the parliament in England and have a prominent clock

The Americanization of Parliament

(Little Ben) that strikes the hours loudly to try to keep the Senate awake.

The Canadian view of the U.S. federal government is that it occupies a bunch of Greek- and Roman-style temples called Washington, D.C. The one with the rose garden and the horse saddled and ready in the back yard is the White House. The White House is where the president of the United States lives and works when his wife is not having it redecorated.

The president's job is to sit on the executive branch and saw it off. Helping him do this is the House of Representatives, whose duties are to

- form more committees than the Russians
- rent hotel suites where congressmen entertain Arab princes who turn out to be FBI agents
- introduce legislation that the president vetoes
- veto legislation that the president introduces
- support the Washington Redskins by wearing a hog snout if they don't already have one.

The other federal legislature that sees its duty as not getting along with the president is the Senate. All U.S. senators speak with a southern accent, wear Stetson hats, and are quite fearless in defending military contracts for their home state.

Despite this brave show of republicanism, many Americans are closet monarchists. They secretly miss George the Third. Fat and dull though he was, as an insensitive collector of taxes he did have more charm than the Internal Revenue Service. Hence the great excitement in the States when Grace Kelly married Prince Rainier. There was hope that the union of the house of Monaco with the house of Philadelphia would produce a Palace with a better class of vaudeville.

Americans have a yearning for pomp and circumstance and spectacle that is only partly satisfied by Macy's Christmas parade. Millions of American women envy Princess Diana because she had a wedding that in the U.S. can be afforded by no one but a Mob godfather.

The life of the parties

Most Americans don't understand Canadian political parties. Neither do most Canadians. Here the similarity ends, however.

To most Americans a Progressive Conservative is a Republican without the staunch. They believe that the PC supports the capitalist system but can't make up his mind about motherhood or apple pie. He opposes the Liberals, for whom love is never having to say you're Tory.

Americans see the Liberal as a Democrat whose brakes failed. The Liberals introduced unemployment insurance, to ensure that most of the people were unemployed. Liberals are harmful because they do things to make Canada different from the United States, such as putting French on boxes of cornflakes.

Heaven punishes Liberalism by making its prime

How we face reality

ministers either bachelors or husbands of women who fool around a lot. Only the States has a First Lady that is covered by a four-year warranty.

Americans have a dim apprehension of the New Democrat as a Bolshevik who has shaved his whiskers off. What their own government would do, in the event that the New Democratic Party seized power in Canada, depends on whether the Rideau Canal is deep enough to receive a U.S. destroyer.

Canadians don't care much for either of the major political parties in the United States because the presidential nomination conventions preempt Bugs Bunny. They know that instead of New Democrats the U.S. has Old Democrats, donkeys who graze on mountains of green stamps. The Democrat is more peaceable than the Republican, but it is still hard to visualize a 200-pound dove.

Republicans are hawks that have played football in college, causing them now to lean to the right. They are more likely to believe in a supernatural power than the Democrats, who draw their strength from the Teamsters Union. The party suffered a big setback when Jimmy Hoffa disappeared; he was the only one who knew the combination to the safe.

The other name for the Republicans is the GOP, which stands for Grand Old Profit. Its symbol is the elephant. Under President Ronald Reagan the elephant never forgets but it has to be reminded a lot.

God a Republican

The Republicans assign to God a large role in U.S. foreign policy. The difference between a freedom fighter and a rebel terrorist in another country is something that God only knows. This assures Him of a place among the president's foreign-policy advisers. The reason why President Reagan spends so much time on his California ranch, despite the brush fires, is that he expects God to speak to him from a burning bush.

Americans detest communism because it is Godless. To Canadians, God is negotiable. Communist atheism doesn't bother Canadians much, so long as it contributes to poor wheat crops in the Soviet Union. If exports of Canadian grain to the U.S.S.R. fall off because the Reds have learned to grow Godless wheat,

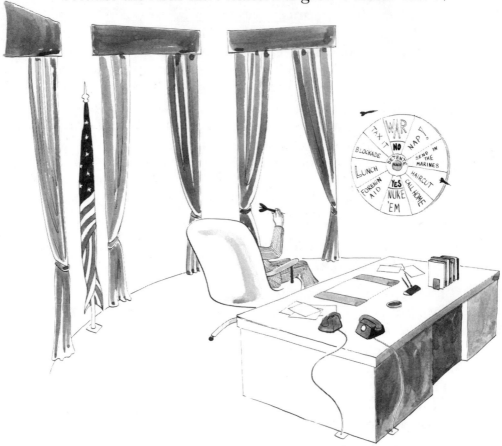

In America, important decisions are made in the Oval Office . . .

Canada will loathe communism as much as the Americans.

Meantime, Canadians restrict their religious fervour to domestic matters. They pray once a week: "Thank God it's Friday!"

. . . the only Canadian equivalent is the Offal office

The Canadian's vision of the U.S. border

The American's vision of the Canadian border

51

Chapter Four

Can-Am Sport, or How Green Is My Bush League?

Le pas de corporate sponsor

The Canadian Football League is contemplating an opening-day ceremony in which the prime minister will throw out the first drunk.

Beer-drinking among the spectators is one of the few aspects of professional sport in which Canadians excel Americans. The average Canadian football fan spills more than the American consumes. Sociologists offer several explanations for Canadians' superior performance in barfing in the bleachers:

1. Alcohol helps the Canadian fan forget how much the American player is being paid.
2. Canadian beer has more bench strength.

3. Even the Dixie cup is an import.
4. Canadian youth programs emphasize throwing up.

At one time professional drinking at major-league games was excused as necessary for the spectator to avoid refrigeration. However, under domes such as Vancouver's B.C. Place Stadium the drinkers have been more unruly than in the old outdoor parks. It has been found necessary to set aside a whole section of seats as a No Puking zone.

This indicates that the malaise of the Canadian pro-sport fan goes deeper than his finding that he has sat on a wad of bubblegum. To be naturally intoxicated is harder when watching a Canadian major-league team that has no Canadians on it. Home games of the Montreal Expos and the Toronto Blue Jays recall those at Rome's Colosseum, where neither the lions nor the Christians were local boys.

Canadian brewers and distillers help to support professional sport in Canada because having a major-league team is how the citizens know that they live in a world-class city. Rural Canadians drink in order to support national teams. And every Canadian-sport patriot says, "I regret that I have but one liver to give for my country."

The survival of Canadian professional sport depends on the ability of the country's spirituous beverages to win against world competition. The Molson bottle has been "capped" several times, as an international. Canadian Club has a winning record against American clubs. With more emphasis on training the minors, Alberta could be successful enough against the Russians to win a gold medal for Canadian vodka.

(*Note*: Canadian drama and music and other performing arts rely more on the tobacco industry to preserve the nation's culture. Some playwrights feel guilty about writing plays — especially comedies — that promote lung cancer. In Canadian ballet, The Dying Swan is suffering from emphysema.)

American major-league sport is less dependent on the prosperity of bad habits. There are several reasons for this, any of which may be right:

(a) Avon provides ladies' tennis with an athletic support.

(b) American pro-team owners are not only multi-millionaires but masochists who get a thrill out of watching their team lose money.

(c) In the States, the Tooth Fairy really puts out. This is why Canadian hockey players prefer to play for American NHL teams: the broken tooth put under the pillow is replaced with U.S. funds.

In some esoteric sports, such as curling, Canadians have won world championships without the financial help of anyone more harmful to health than Air Canada. But curling, like darts and sex, is still viewed as being more a participation sport than one that draws large crowds into bowls.

Premature celebration

It may also say something about the Canadian character that the nation's athletes seem to do best in activities that do not require a lot of teamwork, such as pistol shooting, rhythmic gymnastics, and belly-whopping. More often than not, the Canadian world champion is something of a loner. When he makes a good play, he has to pat himself on the bottom. Or, worse, leap into a joyful embrace of his own body — a manoeuvre that can end his career.

As a manifestation of megalopolis, however, every Canadian city worth its salt corrosion aspires to be part of a major league that has teams in the large cities of the U.S. If the Canadian team actually wins some games, that is a bonus. But the main status symbol is the *franchise*. Having a major-league franchise automatically relegates all the other Canadian cities that don't have one. These become "bush." At this writing, Vancouver, for instance, is still largely bush because it has no major-league baseball team. Semi-bush too are Edmonton, Calgary, Winnipeg, and Halifax. Ottawa may fancy itself as being not far from civilization, but the nation's capital too is mostly impenetrable jungle. It is inevitable that Ottawa defers to Washington, D.C., as the U.S. capital has the Redskins, an NFL football team to which any member of Ottawa's CFL team will defect at the drop of a punt.

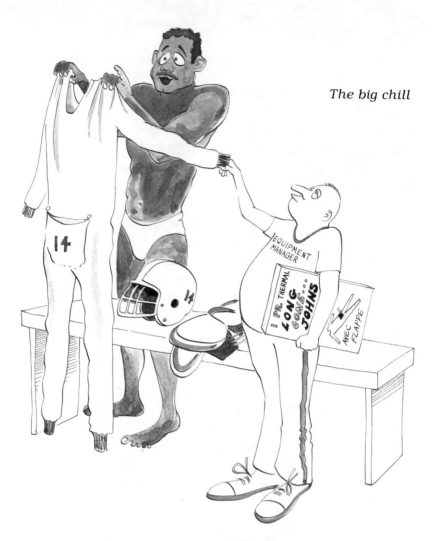

The big chill

Purgatory is the pit stop to Heaven

How does the American football player express his delight at being signed by a Canadian Football League team, after being cut by the National Football League? He tells the media that:

1. He likes the larger Canadian field because it gives him a chance to run from the disappointment.
2. He finds less racial prejudice in Canada, even though he has to ride in the back of the ambulance.
3. He prefers the Canadian dollar since the Queen is prettier than George Washington.
4. He loves hunting and fishing on days when he is not in traction.

How does the American, or the Canadian, football player respond when he plays so well in the CFL that he gets an offer to play third-string in the NFL? He tells the media:

Goodbye.

In Canadian football, the prodigal son is by adoption. The fans are resigned to the fact that the return of the conquering hero is made possible by his failing to make an American team.

If we're not near the one we love . . .

. . . we'll love the one we're near. If a Canadian city doesn't have a major-league team of its own, it roots vicariously for the team of the Canadian city nearest. For westerners, in baseball this means the Toronto Blue Jays. Traditionally, Toronto has been regarded by westerners as:

- Canada's answer to rectal itch
- the only metropolis in the world that combines the spiritual values of Las Vegas with the pizazz of Vatican City
- a Mecca that all devout Canadians face at sunset, to retch.

The Blue Jays have changed that image. If the team ever makes it to the World Series, against an American team, the whole country will be cheering for the Toronto team of Americans shivering in the chill of an Ontario fall. If the Blue Jays lose the World

That remote possibility

Series, the rest of Canada can go back to hating Toronto with a clear conscience.

What if the Blue Jays and the Expos should meet in the World Series? Not having a U.S. city to act as opposition, the series would divide Canadians into (a) anglophones and francophones, (b) Protestants and Catholics, (c) pedestrians and cab drivers. An all-Canadian World Series is dreaded by the U.S. television networks, especially if it is played in snow. Quite aside from the game having to be played with a red or green ball, and relief pitchers having to be brought in from the bullpen by snowmobile, the American viewers' skeletal interest in an all-Canadian World Series would be a mortal blow to the ratings. The White House would be under immediate pressure to:

(a) have Ontario health authorities quarantine the Blue Jays because of psittacosis;
(b) ask Canada to cancel the series till more medical research can be done on herpes as caused by frozen tobacco spit;
(c) confiscate Joe Garagiola's ear muffs;
(d) annex Canada;
(e) threaten to have The Chicken (a Canadian) served as Shake 'n' Bake.

How to increase the Canadian content of Canadian pro sport

1. Include steroids in all school lunches.
2. Shorten the time it takes Cuban exiles to get their citizenship papers. (Suggested period: 15 minutes.)
3. Develop a baseball shaped like a rubber disc and struck with a bladed stick, if the player can't find anything else to hit with.
4. Coach pitchers to adapt their screwball to a 60-mile-an-hour wind.

5. Outbid American colleges offering athletic scholarships, by throwing in a two-week, all-expenses-paid holiday with the dean's wife.

There are some major-league sports that Canadian nationals cannot crack. The National Basketball Association, for example, has recruited few French Canadians despite their title of "the white niggers of North America." It is now too late to import slaves from the Watusi tribe in Africa, the tall warriors having got a smart agent.

Hopes must therefore be directed towards persuading the Americans to change the rules of basketball somewhat, to accommodate the Canadian physique. Namely:

- lower the basket to sea level
- offset the advantage of having long arms by requiring that the ball be carried between the legs
- change the playing surface to ice
- ban the slam dunk as violating the ionosphere.

Many U.S. athletes owe their superiority over Canadians to their having fought their way out of the ghetto, to find refuge in contact sports as professional football players, boxers, and stand-up comedians. In this respect Canada is disadvantaged. The country has relatively few black ghettoes. The white ghettoes don't offer a youngster the special sprint training afforded by mugging an old lady in the street, because these ghettoes are occupied mostly by bums too old to learn the basics of broken field running. The youngster does not develop naturally from stealing hubcaps to stealing second base.

Too many of Canada's juvenile delinquents are lost from professional sport because they can borrow Dad's car. Solution:

1. Reduce the Canadian kid's allowance till he starts to show real ability in jumping fences.
2. Replace the Little League with sandlot baseball, disqualifying any player who wears shoes.
3. Change sex education to define *desire* as something a person must have to make the team — *collectively*.
4. Organize a youth exchange program with the Dominican Republic: ten rock bands in exchange for a good shortstop.

Chapter Five

Libido — A Town in Texas?

Culture shock: California

ost Canadians see Americans as being oversexed. They have watched the Playboy Channel, TV documentaries showing how Americans swim upstream to spawn in Hugh Hefner's pool. They look at the difference in populations — 250 million versus 25 million — and wonder how Uncle Sam finds time to get out of bed.

Conversely, Americans can't imagine the Canadian as being sexed at all. They envisage the hazards of making love on a dog sled, and see the maple leaf as a fig leaf that has nothing to hide. When it comes to multiplying, what the Canadian pulls out of his pants is a pocket calculator.

Meanwhile, back at the raunchy . . .

In the States the mating season lasts from the Super Bowl (January) right through to the World Series (October). In fact the American is almost continually in rut, except for a brief interval to change to winter tires and do Christmas shopping.

For the Canadian, mating season is much shorter. By the time the weather has warmed enough for the male to start losing his winter coat, he has forgotten what the zipper is for. He is barely into his courting dance when his canals freeze up again. Because survival often depends on his long johns, some Canadian women have as many as six children by a man they know only as "Stanfield."

Canadians envy the Americans for their being able to devote more of their waking hours to sexual techniques. To a Canadian, foreplay means dropping his gloves. Canadian female activists used to carry placards saying MAKE LOVE, NOT WAR — till they found out it was quibbling.

Canadian women often find American men more attractive. (Any man looks taller when he is not standing up to his knees in muskeg.) They envy the American woman because

- on the beaches of California and Florida, the men carry their live bait in a bikini, not a bucket
- American men shave closer, making it easier to distinguish the love bite from acupuncture
- in Canada, there is less chance of being widowed by a falling coconut.

70

Canadian men indulge in sex fantasies about the American woman because

- she looks like the girl next door, without the moustache
- the American woman does not go directly from puberty into the menopause
- she knows how to be sexually aggressive without exciting the UN General Assembly.

Canada's trade deficit in sex goddesses, gorgeous hunks, and dreamy what's-its

Canada imports more sex symbols than she exports. This despite the Canadian Development Corporation. Whatever it is that the CDC has been developing, it doesn't steam your glasses.

The United States is the main country with which Canada has a severe imbalance of trade in sex objects. The only Canadian sex object known abroad is a rubber product that rarely appears on the cover of *Time*. Efforts to make singer Anne Murray competitive, as an exported sex goddess, have largely failed. Processors were unable to remove entirely the wholesomeness. This impurity is to blame for Canada's being a heavy importer of oomph. Including that from Japan. (Many Canadians build their sex life around the Mazda ZZZ.)

Even using robots, the Canadian sex-symbol industry has not kept up with the turnover of Liz Taylor's husbands. Many Canadian girls have been centre-

71

folds, but they are lost without the staple. The general rule is: When a Canadian woman is photographed in the nude, it's because her doctor has ordered X-rays.

Only partly wrong are those Canadians who think that erotica is a skin condition, an itch that you can't scratch. Canadian women lust vicariously for American sex objects like Frank Sinatra, Paul Newman, and Neil Diamond, but at home they expect a man to come on like a grain elevator.

When a Canadian woman gets an obscene phone call, she can assume that it is long distance. It was inevitable that the telephone would be invented by an adoptive Canadian (Alexander Graham Bell), since it enabled intimacy without getting too close.

Hairy American rock bands touring Canada have no difficulty attracting groupies, but when the RCMP Musical Ride visits the States there is no relief from sexual tension, for man or beast. The only Canadian male celebrity who regularly finds women waiting for him in U.S. cities is hockey star Wayne Gretzky, who prefers to remain faithful to the team bus.

The porn exchange — why Canada buys No. 1 hard

Although classified as an industrial nation, Canada lags badly in production of pornography. Filth flows north from the States in much greater volume than the trickle of titillation that is Canada's gross national product. Despite the vigilance promised in the

national anthem ("We stand on guard for thee"), thee is up to thy knees in sleaze — made in the U.S.A.

Pornographic magazines and films produced in Canada have been unable to compete with high-tech arousal. Americans refuse to buy X-rated Canadian video cassettes, because they can't be inserted without a vibrator.

Why does this disparity exist, in a trade estimated to be worth billions of dollars and delivered in a plain, brown envelope? Some explanations:

1. Canadians are commercially impotent. They can't penetrate the market for pornography, even though they watch the Americans doing it to them every night.
2. Canadians have no talent for pornography. They think that kinky sex means fondling a pretzel.
3. And that a French kiss is on both cheeks.
4. Parliamentary committees on pornography have found that the Canadian is also confused about prostitution, because the red light goes on *before* he has scored.

As a result of this lack of expertise in carnal hardware, Canadian sex boutiques depend almost entirely on imports. Canadian sex aids, such as the rubber nose for Inuit lovers, have limited appeal in the States. The inflatable doll made by a Canadian tire company failed to catch on because it had to be taken to a service station to be pumped up. And there

Can-Porn

were few takers for the vibrating bed that depended on a spin-dry cycle.

Which way to the obscenic route?

Various recommendations have been made by groups studying ways and means to improve Canada's export of porn to the States.

> *Specialization*: Canada should produce hard-core films of sexual violence that is degrading to moose.
> *Supplying pornograph components*: duck feathers, barbed wire, edible garterbelts, leather harnesses complete with stirrups and a Mountie hat.
> *Funding research*: Is the chain saw being wasted on trees? Can American film producers be encouraged to shoot their skin flicks in Canada, by removing the federal tax on cordage? By replacing Medicine Hat with a hot tub?

The only other hope, in Canada's competing with American-made pornography, is the total victory of the Liberty Federation (formerly the Moral Majority) movement in the States. Already the Reagan return to traditional values has revived the buttoned fly. The comeback of virginity is something that Canada can cash in on. The market may soon be ripe, for example, for a chastity belt that is opened by slipping a plastic ID card into the slot. Canadians must be ready to jump, with the swing from rude to prude. To the pendulum, or the pit?

Chapter Six

Education — Falling between Two Schools

Maintaining Canadian educational standards

Subway graffiti in the States has reached
new . . . er . . . heights

In Canada, subway graffiti is in its infancy

★★★
★★★
★★★
★★★
★★★
★★★
★★★
★★★
★★★
★★★n both Canada and the
States, formal education is what the kid gets in
dressing for the grad party.

The grad party is the term's longest sustained
period of learning, lasting from dusk to the break of
Dad. During this immersion course the student ab-
sorbs most of his sex education, learns the art of the
aerosol graffito, gets physical training in drinking
without upchucking on a rented tux, and is introduced to the reality of terror, seen in the faces of his
parents as they realize that he won't be going off to
school any more.

Relative degrees of tutorial technology, or Goodbye, Mr. Microchips

In the classrooms of both countries, the teacher is the computer. There may be an adult human hanging around the front of the class, but he or she is there mostly to deal with an unruly tape. The principal of the school is an audio-visual aid. That is, at the beginning of the term he or she appears once, in full view of the parents, to explain that this year, because of budget cuts, the field trips will not include students.

Because the U.S. is wealthier than Canada, the school equipment is likely to be more advanced.

- In American schools, chalk is used only at the pool table.
- In Canadian schools, Meet the Teacher Night is supported by Oxfam. The teacher tells the parents to make sure that the student brings a good, nutritious lunch, as well as something to eat himself.
- American high-school football teams are as fully equipped as the pros. With the Canadian high-school football team, the smallest player gets chosen as the ball.
- At U.S. colleges, the walls hold up the *ivy*.
- Canadian schools are subject to brain drain. Luckily, the drain backs up often enough to maintain the level of American professors.

What makes George Washington High?

Both American and Canadian high schools restrict corporal punishment to what happens to the teachers. Some U.S. schools, in the Detroit area, impose longer periods of detention — up to 25 years.

The growing popularity of private schools in Canada shows that many wealthy Canadians want their sons and daughters to experience the British tradition, namely, that the way to establish a seat of learning is to birch it. Americans prefer to put their children into military uniform, at school, so that if the discipline proves too stringent the kid can be buried with full military honours.

American students start the school day by pledging allegiance to the flag. The only time a Canadian student puts his hand over his heart is when he is trying to find his pulse.

At the university level, professors in both countries believe in the supreme being: Tenure.

Evolution is more controversial in Socials classes in the U.S. Canadian teachers make it easier for their students to believe that man is descended from a monkey. They do this by nit-picking and working for peanuts. No teacher mentions Adam and Eve, because then every kid in the class brings him an apple.

Canadian educators complain that learning is distorted by the prevalence of American textbooks in the schools. They insist that Canadian publishers of textbooks can leave just as much white space on a

81

In America, university degrees may be purchased

page as American publishers, without crowding the wordy bits. Because of American books, Canadian students learn that:

- Canada was formed by the last ice age, after which things slowed down.
- Geographically, Canada is smaller than the United States, unless we include the parts that don't count.
- In climate, Canada is one big cold front, waiting to descend on the States and ruin the crops. Temperatures are colder because they come from Celsius, a miserable place in the Yukon.

In Canada, degrees are given in Celsius

- John A. Macdonald was an explorer who discovered the source of American whiskey.
- The Canadian Pacific Railway was built to take unfair advantage of American trains, which had to stop at stations.
- Confederation was started by a group of Confederate soldiers who were sore losers.

Philosophies of education, or how to interface with ignorance

Canadian education has been strongly influenced by American philosophies of education, which are car-

83

ried north on the prevailing winds of change and dumped on unsuspecting school boards, causing genetic damage to the brain. Mutations occur so quickly among these philosophies of education that the basics change into electives, and back again, before the teacher can put on his flak jacket.

The recent economic recession modified the current philosophy of education in the U.S. by eliminating frills. Canadian educators followed suit, by looking for a cheap frill. The Americans returned to the three Rs. This confused the Canadian educators, who don't know their Rs from a hole in the wall. Research is continuing.

Chapter Seven

The Military — Is Canada Being Defensive about Attack?

The little U.S. missile that wasn't there

When the mother of Canada's Achilles dipped him, as a baby, into the Ottawa River, to make him invulnerable in battle, she didn't hold him by the heel. What she *did* hold him by has made him vulnerable to pornography. And the rest of the Canadian Achilles has played it safe by staying out of battle unless it is a really bad night for TV.

Canada's military posture against nuclear attack is based on being the last to know. There is a red telephone in the prime minister's office, but the White House end of the line is in the laundry room.

The U.S. defence headquarters, the Pentagon, was built with five sides, the extra being the side that God is on. In contrast, Canada's defence HQ is round and often taken for a public phone booth, which in fact it is. Canadian chiefs of staff take turns waiting for the phone call from Washington telling them that World War III has started without them.

In addition to this War Room in Ottawa, Canada has a senior officer attached to NORAD headquarters inside a mountain at Colorado Springs, U.S.A. This Canadian officer is given a key when he comes on duty to relieve the American senior officer. The Canadian officer's key is different in that it is the key to the washroom. In the event of a Soviet attack on North America, the Canadian officer goes straight to the washroom and relieves *himself*.

Besides the Distant Early Warning System built in northern Canada to monitor the end of civilization, Canada has its own Better Late Than Never System (BLTNS). The BLTNS consists of a couple of Canadian Armed Forces bases which, in the event of World War III, will suddenly notice the presence of U.S. nuclear weapons. The standing orders then call for the commanding officer to exclaim "Goodness me, where did these nuclear mines come from?" Or "An MX missile? Golly, I thought there was nothing in that silo but corn cobs."

Although U.S. nuclear weapons are frowned on in Canada in peace time, the Distant Early Warning System faces the wrong way to pick up the arrival of

88

American nukes from the south. Also, the missiles are delivered by post office trucks, which move too slowly to be detected by radar.

How Canada can help to make peace compulsory

Has Canada already helped the U.S. to test the so-called Star Wars defence system of laser beams in Canadian air space? Such is indicated by the fact that a Manitoba duck hunter shot down a mallard that was already cleaned, stuffed, and cooked.

Canada has led the arms race in space. That is, it built the arm for the U.S. space shuttle. To be effective in intercepting Soviet missiles, the arm will need to be lengthened somewhat, and fitted with a hockey goalie's blocker. Although net-minder Billy Smith has been seconded to the U.S. defence department, experts doubt that the arm can be taught to hold a stick and slash at the enemy.

Cannon fodder, enriched with Vitamin C

Whereas the U.S. is geared for *nuclear* war, Canada concentrates on *conventional* war, the kind of action that happens at a convention. The Canadian Authors Association convention, for example. The skirmishing around the salad bar can be brutal. But Canada has a proven capability in taking on thousands of Shriners, including their mobile units of tricycles. Should the Soviets try to overwhelm North America

U.S. Air Force war games

Canadian air force games

with a massive international convention of vodka salesmen, the Royal York is just one of several reinforced bunkers built to subdue the offensive force, routing the foe with the loss of only a few hundred towels.

As for NATO, Canada's main role will be to provide human waves of infantry, charging against impregnable positions. Canadian Armed Forces recruits are taught that it is blessed to die for the Ayatollah Reagan. The soldier killed on a suicide mission, trying to hip-check Russian tanks, goes straight to Paradise. There he will enjoy Eternity, being waited upon by beautiful houris serving Betty Crocker's angel cake.

Nevertheless, the basic training of Canadian servicemen takes longer than that of Americans. Reason: the young Canadian is so used to marching for peace that it takes him some time to get used to carrying something on his shoulder other than a placard saying NUCLEAR WAR CAN RUIN YOUR DAY. He expects any advance to stick to main streets, and end up at the U.S. consulate.

Once engaged in combat, however, the Canadian soldier is the equal of the American, provided that the bartender remains neutral.

Taking Candu from a baby

Although Canadians have a low potential as a warlike people, being rated fourth after the Swedes, the Swiss, and the Salvation Army, they worry the U.S. by sell-

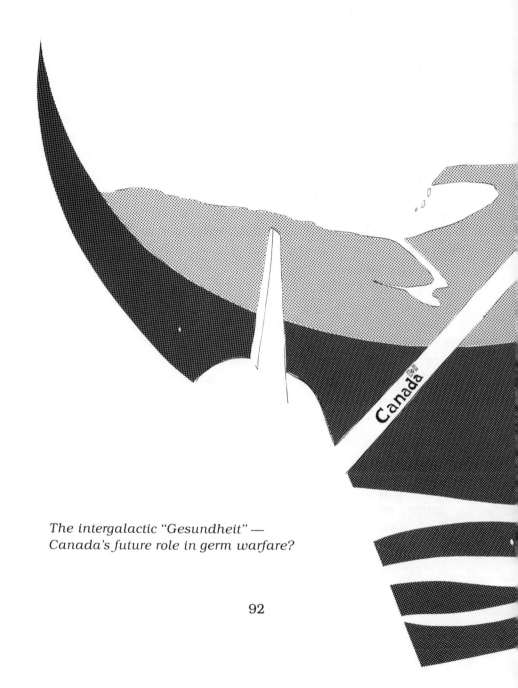

The intergalactic "Gesundheit" —
Canada's future role in germ warfare?

92

ing their Candu nuclear power plant to emotionally unstable nations. The Canadian government has been quietly asked by Washington to be suspicious if the order for a nuclear power station specifies:

1. Racing stripes and the Arabic for "Take that!"
2. The plant's staff cafeteria can be quickly replaced by a long-range missile.

3. A warranty that covers the first 5000 miles, or 20 minutes, whichever comes first.

Question: How may Canada become militarily independent of the United States?

Answer: Germ warfare. Because of the universality of Canada's system of medicare, everyone in the country has been sick with something, building up enormous immunity. The nation is therefore favoured to invent a doomsday bug, a virus that can give the entire population of the U.S., or any other country, a bad case of the trots in a matter of hours. The superpowers have tried to ban germ warfare because it is cheap. Surely, however, the Canadian government can be depended upon to find a way to make it expensive. But it must hurry. Mexico may already have the weapon.

Chapter Eight

We Are What They Eat

★ ★ ★ ★ ★
★ ★ ★ ★ ★ ★ ★
★ ★ ★ ★ ★ ★ ★
★ ★ ★   ★ ★ ★
★ ★ ★
★ ★ ★ ★ ★ ★ ★
★ ★ ★ ★ ★ ★ ★
★ ★ ★   ★ ★ ★
★ ★ ★ ★ ★ ★ ★
★ ★ ★ ★ ★ ★ astronomically, Canada is an American fast-food outlet that missed the curve. In the rapid consumption of junk food, Canadians cannot keep up with Americans. (See overleaf.)

The Canadian meal — an American snack

A few Canadians have a fridge as large as the Americans'. It's called Labrador. The light goes on when they open the Gulf of St. Lawrence.

Americans eat more meat than do Canadians, especially beef. In some parts of the U.S. West, ordering a quarter-pounder is considered to be effeminate. Canadians dining in American restaurants are

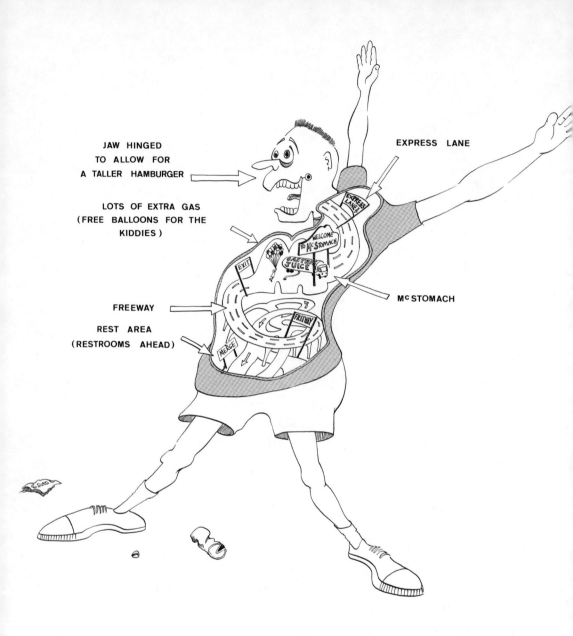

American junk-food addict's digestive system

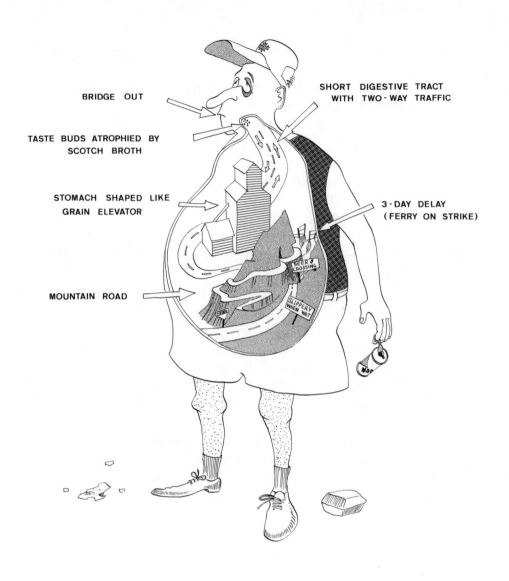

Canadian junk-food addict's digestive system

often embarrassed because Father's hernia pops when he picks up their doggie bag. The American restaurant is unique in having the only dessert cart with truck suspension. What a Nova Scotian calls a roast, the Texan calls a steak. What the Texan calls a roast, a Nova Scotian tries to milk.

The Canadian diner does not go into shock if he is able to see part of his plate. Canadians rarely live to eat. What they *do* live for is a mystery, but it probably needs ketchup.

Because Americans have historically, as emigrants from the Old World, associated poverty with hunger and starvation, they make sure that their poor are the fattest in the world. Their poverty line is much thicker than the Canadian. A completely destitute American can be enormous. One reason why the poor do not rise up against the U.S. government is that they have trouble heaving themselves out of the chair.

In Canada there is less obesity among the poverty-stricken, because the government does not insist that they have food. Canadians are not pressured by green stamps. They are free to spend their welfare cheques on other necessities of life, namely liquor and tobacco. As a result the Canadian poor are less overweight than the underprivileged in the States, where it takes only two people to make a crowd.

If one sees a very thin American, one knows that he, and especially she, is wealthy. Americans are assured that theirs is the richest nation on earth when the president's wife looks emaciated. Canadian prime ministers too have had very slim wives in recent years, but this was because the prime ministers were rich, not the country. To be truly representative of the amount of starch in the Canadian diet, Mila Mulroney should put on about ten pounds.

This is why the Russians have had to hide their leaders' wives, right up to Mrs. Gorbachev, who is svelte enough to reflect improved Soviet grain crops.

Starve Wars

The Americans still enjoy a big lead, however, in dropping megapounds of flesh. While portly Russian housewives continue to line up to buy food, the American woman is attending a fitness class to prove that Karl Marx wore a girdle. This fitness craze (which lives off the fad of the land) has spread to Canada. Canadians are strongly influenced by glossy U.S. magazines with photos of gleaming muscle persons who oil their entire body, not just the parts that squeak. Then the Chilcotin cowboy wonders why he keeps slipping off his horse.

Some Canadian women also believe that

- real women do not have breasts — their pecs just have a speed bump
- sexual equality is somehow related to looking as lumpy as a man
- if Jane Fonda is a leftist, Ed Broadbent should look better in tights

Can-American dames

- happiness is being able to bench-press 200 pounds at the gym without lifting a finger around the house
- if the Canadian man wants something soft and Continental to go to bed with, he can buy a Danish quilt.

Revelation is seeing the Lite

Americans have made Canadians very conscious of their diet. Until American doctors started writing bestselling books telling people what to eat, Canadians didn't care what was in their food so long as it didn't wriggle. They never counted the calories, they counted the cutlery. Unless a guest appeared to have swallowed his knife, fork, and spoon, his meal was considered healthful.

Now, carried away on the tide of American calorie-consciousness, the Canadian is a gastronomic Odysseus trying to navigate his body between the Scylla of cholesterol and the Charybdis of carcinogenic additives. He lashes himself to the mast, to avoid going overboard about polyunsaturated fats. From being the foe of tyranny and injustice, the Canadian now concentrates on hating salt.

Canadians have learned from Americans to distrust dairy products. They have mixed feelings about the cow. If Satan has horns and hooves, maybe she also has an udder.

Americans made it chic to drink bottled water. Snobs in Vancouver, which has an abundance of cold, sparkling mountain water coursing from its faucets, promptly began ordering Perrier. They betrayed tap water as Canada's national drink. The French have wine, the Chinese their tea, the Americans coffee, the Russians vodka, but nothing speaks more eloquently of the Canadian character than a tumbler full of clear, minimally chlorinated *aqua pura*,

103

"Perhaps a tad less chlorine . . ."

on the rocks. Yet fancy restaurants no longer serve it unless it is asked for. Nor do they have the national zeal to put eau naturel on the menu with the other beverages, and charge as befits an epicure's delight . . .

"May I suggest, monsieur, 'dame, the aperitif specialty of the house — Liebfrauwasser? The latest in non-alcoholic *boissons*. Drawn direct from alpine streams whose pristine virginity has struck awe into every connoisseur of slowly-melted snow. We recommend that you drink it without adding whisky or other mixer, so that you may appreciate the subtle bouquet of unscaled peaks, the pellucid absence of all colour. And this has been a vintage year, for our water: no one drowned in the intake."

Without this guidance, the American visitor has no concept of Canadian cuisine. If he can imagine a Canadian menu at all, it runs to a combination of British and Eskimo staples.

Watercress and Walrus Soup
Kippered Beluga Whale au Admiral Peary
Pâté de Foie Canada Goose, on a Crumpet

A Canadian gastronomic event: Moose Popover with Rack of Loon (for two)

Yorkshire Pemmican
Hot Pot of Mukluk, Devon Gravy
Moose Popovers
Trolley of Permafrost Sweets
Potted Mountain Goat Cheese
Lousewort Tart
Arctic Bunny Fingers
Iced Tea

Why not accommodation on *the Canadian Plan?*

To distinguish it from the European Plan (hotel room only) and the American Plan (hotel room and meals combined), the Canadian Plan includes meals but no hotel room. Eliminates the NO VACANCY sign that often annoys visitors.

Chapter Nine

Have Some American Media, M'dear

" . . . We see thee rise . . ."

W

hen Canadians appeal to a higher power, they ask Abby. Many Irish Canadians believe that the pope is infallible, but for *real* problems they watch Donahue.

Some other common Canadian beliefs, gained from American media:

- It is impossible to visualize God, but He probably looks something like Walter Cronkite.
- A nuclear war may mean local blackout. Subscribe to Pay-TV.

- The Canadian newspaper demonstrates its intellectual independence by running Doonesbury.
- The New Testament is holy, but *The New York Times* is an authority.
- A foreign correspondent is a reporter based in Ottawa.

Many American newspapers have Canadian content. It comes in large rolls and says a lot about the depletion of Canada's forests. Once the newsprint has gone through the presses, however, Canada loses the American's attention. The only Canadian events that make the news south of the line are:

— CANADA BLOWS ARCTIC FRONT. Freezes Florida oranges.
— RUSSIAN SATELLITE CRASHES IN NORTH. Only 1000 miles from Alaska.
— GRIZZLY EATS AMERICAN TOURIST.
— PRIME MINISTER'S WIFE JOINS ROCK GROUP. "Tired of playing second fiddle."

It is easy for Canadians to know what is an important event in their country: it is reported in *Time* magazine. Canada's national news magazine does not receive the same regard in the States, where *Maclean's* (pronounced "Macleens") is known as a toothpaste. Cavities in their knowledge of current events in Canada are something that Americans can live with.

Disciples of the converter

The geographical proximity of U.S. television to Canada has created five thousand miles of undefended boredom. Yet most Canadians believe that finding new horizons means getting cablevision.

The amount of American TV programs sold to Canadian networks is a tribute to U.S. technology in recycling garbage.

Some Canadians watch CBC programs as a duty, easier to take than compulsory military service. Canadian TV shows must be produced with a much lower budget than those of NBC, ABC, and CBS, which means that instead of climaxing the drama with a violent and destructive car chase, the CBC show extracts as much excitement as possible from the villain's falling off his bicycle. Other variants:

- The American show features glamorous women wearing expensive furs. The Canadian: Just the fur. Usually with the fox still in it.
- American TV: The courtroom scene includes judge and jury and a full crowd of spectators. Canadian TV: Trial by judge only; the judge has ordered the courtroom cleared of all union actors.
- American TV: The hero is a sophisticated, highly computerized muscle car that has an urbane manner of speech. Canadian TV: The hero is a milk wagon. The horse does all the talking.
- American TV: The soaper family lives in a

southern mansion or a large Texas ranch. Canadian TV: All the family crises occur in a closet. Wealth is indicated by having the lovers get into bed wearing yachting caps.

Canadians get much of their sex education from U.S. television. The declining birthrate may be attributed to the TV contraceptive: before the couple making love can attain climax, they go into a commercial. Millions of Canadians think that hugging and kissing lead to spurts of Windex. They are disappointed when sexual intercourse doesn't leave their sink sparkling clean.

For more biologically realistic sex education, thinking Canadians watch the Public Broadcasting Service. Parents who used to mumble to their child about the birds and the bees now simply tell him

TONIGHT ON
THE NATURE
OF STUFF
Spawning
Salmon
of B.C.

KATNIP

"Watch Channel 9." Canadians are proud of Lorne Greene, who has done more for sex education than any other national, by hosting dozens of PBS nature documentaries that show Canadians how to complete the sex act under water, clinging to a tree branch, or simply waiting for an enterprising bird to eat their berry and poop the seed.

In making sex sound academic, Canada remains unexcelled, even by the Americans, in steam radio. The dispassionate objectivity of CBC radio newscasts, rivalled only by that of the BBC, makes it possible for a Canadian to be recognized as an intellectual without his having to learn to read.

Chapter Ten

Culturalism — How the Multi Are Fallen

anada has a federal minister of multiculturalism, whose job it is to watch the cultural mosaic in case the pieces come unstuck. For the nation's birthday (July 1st), he or she gives money to ethnic groups to celebrate what's different about them. The States can't do this on their national day (July 4th), because *United* is part of the country's name. Luckily, there is no such thing as the United Provinces of Canada.

This cultural diversity helps to prevent the arts from becoming too massive in Canada, and presenting a threat to Disneyland.

116

117

It is more blessed to give than to receive . . .

. . . a Canadian book. Many Canadians express their patriotism by buying at least one Canadian book a year. They buy it at Christmas time, to give to someone else. For the remaining 50 or so weeks of the year they buy paperbacks by Robert Ludlum, Sydney Sheldon, and Stephen King. These books they read themselves. They may hate themselves in the morning, but only because they are Canadian authors.

Canadians read American bestsellers when they want mystery, romance, glamour, sex, or violence. They read a Canadian bestseller when they want the history of the Canadian Pacific Railway. This is why the Canadian author usually needs to supplement his or her writing income by:

(a) becoming a preferred customer at a food bank;
(b) marrying his publisher;
(c) reading from her work to high-school students (if she can buy accident insurance from Lloyd's of London);
(d) getting lucky at church bingo;
(e) finding a cheap source of protein other than eating the children.

Because they owe their meagre livelihood to Christmas giving, Canadian authors are under more pressure to believe in Christ than are American authors, who just have to believe in Hollywood. The Canadian author is also kept humble by the pro-

"And how long have you been promoting Canadian culture?"

motional tour, during which he is kept waiting in the studio ante-room while an American author is being interviewed on radio or TV. After a while he comes to identify with the studio's sprinkler system. He refuses to go till someone starts a fire.

Canadian publishers specialize in coffee-table books — large, expensive volumes of colour photos of all the scenic places in Canada where a person would sooner be than waiting in an ante-room. Canadian coffee-table books are bought mostly by the subsidiaries of large American corporations that want to impress the visitor with their devotion to the Ca-

119

nadian wilderness. The coffee-table book also makes the ideal gift for the company executive who is taking early retirement after admitting a sexual preference for Rocky Mountain longhorn sheep.

American publishers produce fewer coffee-table books, pound for pound, and the books are usually photo studies of nude people playing with their shadows.

This makes the books art. Canadians don't trust art, outside a museum. But they do spend a good deal of time in the bookstore, examining American coffee-table books, before deciding that their coffee-table doesn't have it in the legs.

Canadian vs. American art, or Where did everybody go?

The main difference between Canadian and American art is that Canadian painters never paint people. When they paint men and women it is as MEN and WOMEN, on doors where interpretation is not a virtue.

The closest the Canadian artist gets to doing a portrait is to paint a fence post. A weathered prairie fence post is seen as having more personality than a Whistler's Mother, unless her rocker has termites. Van Gogh's self-portrait, minus his ear, would never occur to a Canadian painter, who is more concerned about having his grant cut off.

If an American had painted *The Last Supper*, he would have made it an outdoor barbecue. A Canadian

painter would have concentrated on the table, whose leaves were turning.

The most famous Canadian painter was The Group of Seven. He called himself The Group of Seven to avoid feeling lonesome and ignored by the U.S.

Canada has produced no painter like Norman Rockwell, who painted the faces of America in loving and amusing attitudes. To the Canadian painter the face is one of the private parts. When he wants a professional model, he hires a fishboat.

Arty facts

Canada has more artifacts per square mile than the United States, thanks to the native peoples. After a slow start, the Canadian Eskimo have out-produced the Alaska Eskimo and now dominate the world market for stone carvings of Woman Holding a Fish. British Columbia's West-Coast totem poles are the most sought after because they know how to tell a funny story, often falling over before they can finish it. With the dwindling market for Canadian lumber abroad, the country's best hope is to export more logs to Japan and China in the form of totem poles. If every Chinese family can be sold on having its very own lodge pole in front of the house, instead of TV, the future looks bright for the ancient craft.

The other major Canadian artifact is the telephone. This instrument was invented by a semi-Canadian, Alexander Graham ("Ma") Bell, who anticipated the desire of the Canadian to talk to someone else without having to be near him. Today

Canadians are the world's biggest users of the telephone, although the Americans lead in the technology of getting wrong numbers.

Canada marches to a different humdrum

For any occasion when Canadians are in a festive mood they bring in a Scottish bagpiper who plays till the feeling goes away.

Herein lies the main difference in spirit between Canadian and American music: in New Orleans a jazz band plays "The Saints Go Marching In" preceding the hearse to celebrate a funeral, while at Montreal's Mardi Gras the only wild music heard is when a trumpet player finds that his lips are frozen to the mouthpiece.

The only time a Canadian gets carried away by the music is when he is tolling a church bell.

Canadian music is also more regional than American. In the Maritimes, all dancers wear clogs, to discourage their partner from getting too close. They also keep their arms stiffly at their sides. This contributes to the low birth-rate on the east coast. In Newfoundland, only two musical instruments are known: the fiddle and the harp seal. Newfies use one to stun the other, believing it to be more merciful than using a club. Most Atlantic fiddlers can't read music because the fog is too thick. But their sawing and plucking is just as infectious as that in Nashville, and even more resistant to penicillin.

Them tundra blues

At the other end of the musical scale — grand opera — Canadian composers have been just as successful as American composers, who can't write them either. Much as North Americans enjoy opera, the devotees refuse to get all dressed up in order to listen to someone suffering in English.

Where Canadian music does find a role model is in the American rock band. The illustration overleaf shows the only means of identifying a rock band as Canadian.

Canadian popular music was strongly influenced by Elvis Presley. Until the King came to power,

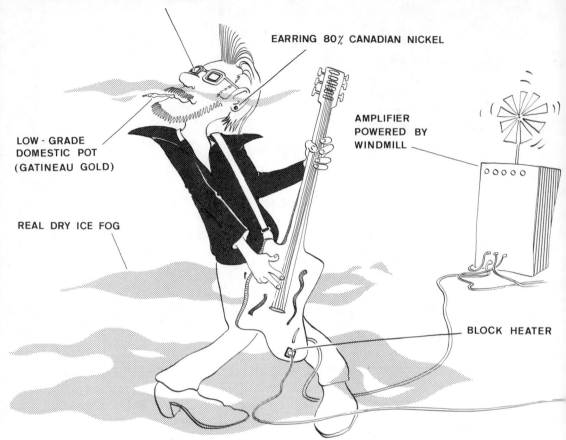

FROST SHIELDS ON DARK GLASSES

EARRING 80% CANADIAN NICKEL

LOW - GRADE DOMESTIC POT (GATINEAU GOLD)

AMPLIFIER POWERED BY WINDMILL

REAL DRY ICE FOG

BLOCK HEATER

Canadian rock star

Canadians thought that it was possible to sing without moving the hips. The normal posture for a Canadian baritone was to hold hands with himself, close his eyes, and think hard about Nelson Eddy. Eddy, though an American, epitomized the RCMP style of rock, namely boulder.

Presley and other American rock idols introduced Canadians to the guitar as a phallic symbol. Previously the only phallic symbol that Canadian music had was the kazoo, which had a limited range of arousal.

Life on the bounding balletomane

Canadian ballet, most critics agree, is every bit as good as the American, because:

1. Long, graceful leaps come naturally to people brought up among Montreal cab drivers.

How Montreal encourages ballet

2. Canadians don't feel self-conscious about wearing long underwear to express the higher emotions.
3. Seizing a girl at the waist and twirling her 'round and 'round is a normal extension of oil drilling in Alberta.
4. Canadians have no trouble understanding ballet in French.

All the world's a stage, but only Broadway counts

It is the ambition of every Canadian playwright to have his play run on Broadway for more than one night. If he can't get his play produced *on* Broadway, he will gladly settle for an off-Broadway production, so long as it is south of the 49th parallel.

Canadian plays in French enjoy more respect in Canada because there is less chance of their eventually going to Broadway and running for only one night. The language barrier keeps out the New York critics unless they have been stranded at Mirabel airport. This absence of the criterion of success in the United States has favoured all French Canadian literature, making the writers more self-assured and less subject to thumb-sucking, bed-wetting, and writing letters to the editor to decry U.S. foreign policy.

The province of Ontario has been affluent enough to overcome the Broadway syndrome by adopting William Shakespeare as a regional playwright of promise. The Stratford Festival provides a splendid setting

Can-Ham

for this playwright, who has been granted landed immigrant status. Shakespeare festivals also occur in the States, but none is as prestigious as that at Stratford, where Canadian plays such as *Hamlet*, *Othello*, and all the polite parts of *Henry IV* have been solid hits. The other popular Ontario playwright is Bernard Shaw, who goes over Niagara Falls regularly without a barrel.

For other new plays, Canadian and American theatre differ as follows:

Canadian plays are usually about poor ethnic farm life. Reason: It costs less to build the set for a play that takes place entirely in a storm cellar. American plays are more likely to be able to afford indoor plumbing. A Canadian musical, however, is built around one girl who can play the harmonica while tapdancing. For an extravaganza, she does it wearing a wig.

As for cast, the monodrama is the most popular kind of Canadian dramaturgy, cutting the cost of the cast to hiring a single performer. Most Canadian artistic directors are looking for the exciting new Canadian play that requires no actors at all. The dramatic action is provided by members of the audience responding to a creative stimulus, such as the stage manager's yelling "Fire!"

American theatrical producers can afford not only larger casts and more elaborate sets, but also costumes made especially for the show. Canadian actors are expected to supply their own costumes. A recent production of *Oedipus Rex* suffered because all the togas were clearly marked PROPERTY OF HOLIDAY INN.

Writing the great Canadian novel

Today the world, tomorrow Canada

Successful American playwrights can afford to live in picturesque old barns in Connecticut. Canadian authors also live in barns, but the cows are still there. Canadian writers wear elbow patches to show that they are literary, and seat patches to prevent being arrested.

Very successful Canadian writers lose no time in moving to New England or California, where they are granted refugee status. They return to Canada occasionally, to inspire other authors to try to escape.

Chapter Eleven

Scratch a Canuck, Find Donald Duck

The American vacationer in Canada

Most Canadians share a religious fanaticism about their annual pilgrimage into the U.S. At sunset, they turn to face Disneyland. In their hegira south they ignore the hardship of an unfavourable exchange rate on the dollar, of motel clerks staring stonily at their Canadian traveller's cheque as though it is a Dead Sea scroll, of suffering, in trailer camps, the sneers of other gypsies because their camper has no jacuzzi.

Canadians take a trip into the States for a variety of reasons:

1. It gives them a lift — especially if they run into a Kansas tornado.
2. They want to see what sand looks like when it is not being shovelled out the back of a city works truck.
3. They can hear "Surf's up!" without having to wait for Father to fall into the bog garden.
4. Risking skin cancer is better than having moss growing on the north side of their trunk.
5. In Canada gambling is a mortal sin, but south of the 49th parallel God allows more latitude.

Americans have had only one reason to visit Canada: to enjoy the great outdoors by killing something. They hope to take home the souvenir of a mounted salmon, a mounted moose head, or a mounted policeman. Lately, however, the blood lust has been found to be less motivating to the American tourist than is the desire to experience a foreign environment. Hence the proposed new Canadian dollar shaped like a beaver turd.

How to domesticate a tourist

Various methods have been suggested to correct the tourist-trade imbalance by keeping the Canadian dollar in the country:

- Put the federal department of tourism under the direction of the man who built the Berlin Wall. Leave Canadians entirely free to visit the

The Canadian vacationer in Canada

States any time they want, if they can make it
across the mine field.
● Turn Alberta into Nevada North, with all kinds
of gambling legal, Calgary being Canada's Vegas and the Lake Louise Hotel the world's biggest glacier-fed brothel.

- Give away bumper stickers: I FOUND JESUS AT HOME.
- Encourage travel agents to promote more bus tours for Canadians to Churchill, Manitoba, to watch the polar bears eat the residents.

Travel is broadening, unless you forgot your lunch

Social intercourse brought on by travel in the U.S. has led to modification of Canadian manners, such as augmenting oral sex with bubblegum.

Thousands of Canadians worry about which is proper etiquette: to hold their dinner fork British-style, in the left hand with the tines down, or to transfer the fork to the right hand like the Americans, gripping it like a Chinese pingpong bat to scoff up the peas.

The Canadian staying at an American hotel commonly leaves his shoes outside his door, upon retiring, and in the morning instead of the shined shoes finds a note saying "How did you know my size? Thanks."

Because of the Americans, Canadians have a colour problem: the American dictionary says the preferred spelling is *color*, their Canadian publisher insists on the British *colour*, and their Japanese word processor loses both spellings and commits Atari kari.

Canadians can help to distinguish themselves from Americans in many small ways:

- Never give the "high five" victory salute. Make it a high four, or better yet wear mittens.
- Avoid loud shirts that look as though they were bought in Honolulu. If unable to resist buying a T-shirt that says I ♡ NY, use it as a tea towel.
- Develop a distinctive Canadian hamburger: a square bun, between two patties of Alberta beef.

"MOOSEHENGE"

THESE EERIE MONOLITHS ARE FOUND THROUGHOUT THE PRAIRIES. HOW THEY CAME TO BE, REMAINS A MYSTERY. IT IS BELIEVED THE ANCIENTS ALIGNED EACH STRUCTURE WITH THE STARS AND THE NEAREST CO-OP STORE.

HISTORIC SITE

- Build a Canadian automobile as nationally prestigious as the Volvo is for Sweden. Call it the Vulva. Pricey, but worth it for the sensational transmission. Make every Arab sheik crave one.

- The fashionable Canadian drug habit, instead of cocaine, is to sniff *real* snow. Have Canadian actors arrested for trying to make a buy from a Zamboni. Sell the stuff to Colombians seeking the thrill of having their sinuses frozen solid.

Besides these minor projects, Canada must construct more historical ruins. American tourists love ruins, the older and mouldier the better. They flock in great numbers to Europe in order to observe the ruins of ancient Greece and Rome and feel better about their playroom. The Colosseum in Rome earns more foreign dollars today than when the Christians got in for nothing.

It is therefore up to Canada to create more historical ruins than are to be seen on the present guided tour of the Senate. Instead of putting a roof on Montreal's Olympic Stadium, it may be more profitable to roll up the rug, tear off part of the walls, and display the hulk to American tourists as the arena where black slaves were torn apart by the Eskimos.

Failure to take these measures to be culturally distinctive may lead to the next chapter.

*American pedestrians: Bostonians exercising their
constitutional rights during rush hour*

Canadian pedestrians

(1) 2:14 P.M.: 3 Torontonians waiting at a stuck "Don't Walk" indicator

*(2) 2:19 P.M.: 5 Torontonians and a pigeon at a stuck
    "Don't Walk" indicator*

(3) 2:26 P.M.: 9 Torontonians, 2 Hamiltonians, a visitor
from Guelph, and 2 pigeons at a stuck "Don't Walk" indicator

(4) 2:38 P.M.: *19 Torontonians, 2 Hamiltonians, 3 visitors from Guelph, 14 schoolgirls from Saskatoon, a farmer from Chicoutimi, a veterinarian from Prince Rupert, 5 basketball players from Antigonish, and 4 pigeons waiting at a stuck "Don't Walk" indicator*

146

*(5) A whole bunch of Canadians unaware that the "Walk"
indicator is finally working*

Chapter Twelve

The Continentalization of Canada

Crazy Sam

The CIA morning stroll in Ottawa, 1990

or NDP leader Ed Broadbent it is his worst nightmare, after being caught in bed with Margaret Thatcher: *The continentalization of Canada.*

Actually Canada was almost continentalized during the mid-century, when American oil companies bought the Canadian exploration rights to everything but the Queen Mother. The Liberals under Trudeau instituted *incontinentalization*. This program consisted of uncontrolled voiding of taxpayers' money, to buy back bits of Canada that the Americans didn't want for prices higher than they were worth.

151

In 1984 the Canadian people got tired of paying inflated rates to retrieve their own resources, and they kicked out the incontinentalizing Grits, giving a massive mandate to the Mulroney government, which immediately set about *disincontinentalization*. This was solemnized with the Shamrock Summit, at which Mulroney and Reagan pledged eternal devotion, with External Affairs Minister Joe Clark acting as flower girl.

As Irish union, the *disincontinentalization* of Canada not only failed to inspire Northern Ireland and Eire to follow the example but also proved shaky once the pope's blessing had worn off. In fact, a group of Canadian nationalists has sought support for the *antidisincontinentalization* of Canada. These zealots see Canada being absorbed by the States, by the process of economic osmosis.

Chronology of the slow leak

1987 — Canadian Senate replaced by a Wendy's. Senators who are found to be alive are given the option of retiring from politics or becoming an old-fashioned hamburger.

1988 — Suspicions are raised by the expansion north of Martha's Vineyard and the coincidental disappearance of Prince Edward Island.

1989 — Canadians elect first NDP socialist government in Ottawa. The White House immediately slaps

152

an embargo on Canada and asks Congress for $100 million for CIA agents to train Progressive Conservative *contras* to wear green berets and blow up Via Rail. The Canadian maple leaf is condemned by Washington as being the Red Star with a stem.

1990 — U.S. guarantees military protection for newly independent province of Saudi Alberta. Trans-Canada Highway sealed off with camel dung.

1991 — Army junta seizes power in Ottawa. Junta led by General Electric. G.E. promises democratic elections in which Canadians can vote for either A.C. or D.C.

1992 — Soviet Union objects to change in Canadian flag to 51 maple leaves and stripes. Moscow accuses the president of the U.S. of acquiring Canada by putting it in her husband's name.

1993 — U.S.S.R. and U.S.A. agree to decide which owns Canada by tossing a coin.

1994 — Geneva talks still deadlocked on whose coin to use.

Activists for Canadian independence admit that Canadians and Americans have a lot in common, namely, acid rain, acid rock, and acid stomach. The Canadian way of life may be simply a matter of adding lime.

But the nationalists insist that Canadians are distinguished by some deeper qualities that don't show up on litmus paper.

153

"Why me?"

What's special about a Canadian, besides the bronze halo?

1. *Canadians are more modest than Americans.* They don't expect to win the gold medal for anything. For Canadians, the streets of Heaven are paved with bronze. When Canada produces a world champion, the people assume:

(a) He or she was born in another country and has been a Canadian citizen for ten days.

(b) The Russians were not competing.

(c) The Canadian team had the wind behind them.

(d) The other contestants had been drinking/ failed the dope test/been taken hostage by terrorists.

(e) All of the above.

Canadians believe that Canada is a nice place to live, but they wouldn't want to visit here. They rarely boast that Canada is the best country in the world, in case someone asks why. Canada produces less raw jingoism than any other land except Tibet. Chauvinism is restricted to the provincial level, where it is displayed on licence plates ("Beautiful British Columbia," "La Belle Province," etc.). Canada is too big to have developed an ego that covers all ten provinces, the territories, and the mayor of Montreal.

2. *Unlike the Americans, Canadians have a great aptitude for remaining neutral.* Canada is a nation of referees. They are trusted by the entire world, when it comes to blowing the whistle. The Canadian salute is one arm held straight up above the head to indicate a penalty. When the UN flag is attached to the arm, Canadian soldiers may ride in a jeep between combatants who are confident that these peacekeepers are backed by massive reserves of disinterest.

In contrast, Americans can't resist taking sides. Being impartial makes them nervous. They are nat-

urally adversarial. Even their baseball umpires indicate a strike or an out by punching the air
belligerently.

Americans are so determined to be the Good Guys
that they will stop at nothing. They are prepared to

kill for human rights. The American says "My country, right or wrong." The Canadian: "My country, but what are the other options?"

The statistical probability of a public-opinion poll asking the question "Are Canadians too noncommittal?":

Yes — 10%
No — 10%
No opinion — 80%

3. *The U.S. is the more virtuous nation, but Canada is decent.* Evidence: The States have been quicker to restore capital punishment. Americans place such a high value on human life that they will kill someone who takes it. Although most Canadians favour the death penalty, parliament is waiting for the States to develop a humane method of execution that won't require the services of a member of the Canadian Medical Association.

Americans show more enterprise in exporting freedom. They are blessed with a surplus of liberty that they are anxious to share with other countries, by force if necessary. Canadians, however, produce only enough human rights to meet their own needs. They are happy if Amnesty International gives them a B-minus. Both countries are generous in their foreign aid, but Canadians are less influenced by whether the applicant people is starving to the right or to the left.

Since Vietnam, Americans have spent much time searching their conscience for possible flaws. They worry about soul erosion. Not so the Canadian. Not being charged with the moral leadership of the Free World, he can devote more time to feeling guilty about morning breath.

4. *Canadians are less volatile than Americans.* It is said that the Canadian is more thoughtful than his city cousin. However, there is no scientific evi-

dence that he is thinking. He may just be standing there, or more likely sitting there, possibly lying there, without any measurable mental activity.

Canadians see Americans as prone to spontaneous combustion. To Americans, Canadians are proof that the rule "Everything in moderation" can be carried to excess. As cold-blooded as a vertebrate can get and still suckle its young. Canadians are ideal candidates for cryogenic intergalactic space travel, requiring a minimum of adjustment to being bodily frozen for release at a more convenient time.

For their part, Canadians fear that union with the U.S. may leave them with a lowered resistance to hysteria. They accept the article of faith that God saw that the world needed a Valium, so He created Canada.

As for the few Americans who have considered the absorption of the northerners into their nation, they feel some apprehension about taking 25 million tranquillizers without knowing the possible side-effects.

In Canada, there are two languages

In America, there is only one language — Money

In Canada, things may be done twice: In French, then English, or Things may be done twice in Canada: In English, then French

162

In the States things are done once

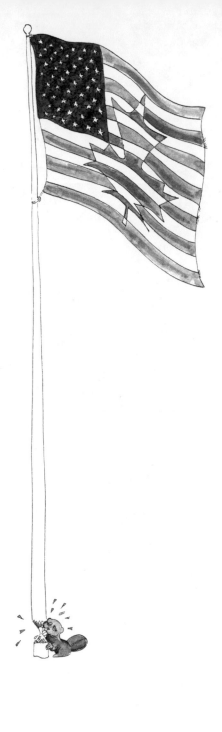

Chapter Thirteen

Do We Conclude with "God Bless Americanada"?

Is it Canada's future to be a sort of hydrocephalic Puerto Rico? Or will the country retain its sovereignty, refusing to give up its locker in the Commonwealth Club?

First, the global overview. The rest of the world will object to political union of Canada and the U.S. because:

1. The U.S. is already too big for its cowboy boots. Geographically, Americanada will be the largest country on earth. It will make the continent of North America top-heavy. Squishing Mexico and Central America into a banana pudding.

2. The U.S.S.R. will demand that the marriage be annulled. On the grounds that the bride was raped before, during, and after the service.
3. The United Nations Organization will deplore the loss of an original-member country (Canada) with such a long and enviable record of abstaining from voting.

Domestically, Americanada spells doom for Ottawa, whose federal function is usurped by Washington, D.C. The scenario: The Ottawa River is clogged with the bodies of civil servants, suicides, bureaucrats who preferred to die rather than lose their seniority. Many flee across the bridge to Hull, Quebec, desperately trying to remember their French irregular verbs. Quebec rejects the union with the U.S., after the Americans refuse to make either Congress or cornflakes bilingual. It is reinstated as a colony of France, exchanging the Montreal Canadiens hockey team for a French atomic bomb.

In playing the strings of free trade with the U.S., the Canadian government is like the male black widow spider wooing the much larger female: the trick is to get her tied up in silken trade agreements long enough for him to screw her and get the hell out before she can eat him. Poor footwork can be fatal. This is why most Canadian federal governments have chosen to emulate the male spider who spends a lot of time on feasibility studies, then takes a cold shower.

The mortal embrace can happen only if the various Canadian provinces become emotionally involved with greed:

- British Columbia deepens her affair with California, finding that she can sell the state more natural gas if someone caps the House of Commons.
- Alberta ranchers persuade the province to get hitched to Idaho, forming an axis of meat and potatoes.
- Saskatchewan and Manitoba remain shacked up together, asserting that they are the only real, friendly people in the country, and trespassers will be shot.
- Ontario elopes with New York State. After years of yearning for the fleshly delights of Buffalo, across the lake, the prim province succumbs to being ravished on the shared waterbed.
- Quebec rents the province to Renault, as a car park.
- The three Maritime provinces live commonlaw with New England, converting the fish canneries into steam baths for gay Mainers.
- Newfoundland admits that she is frigid, and becomes a stationary aircraft carrier for the U.S. Navy.

"Eh Canada?"

The national anthem, "O Canada," as amended by the Mulroney government in preparation for trade talks with the U.S., Canadian Indians, and a Japanese schoolboy named Miki Suki, who wants to trade his Scout knife for Canada's lumber industry.

Eh Canada?
  Our home and native land![1]
True patriot loot[2]
  To all thy persons[3] hand.
With glowing eyes[4]
  We see thee rise,
The True South[5]
  Strong and free!
From dum-de-dum[6]
  Eh Canada,
We stand on God[7] for thee.
God help[8] our land
  When trade is free![9]
Eh Canada,
  We stand on God for thee.
Eh Canada,
  What will be in it for me?[10]

1. This does not represent government acceptance of aboriginal land claims.
2. "Love" will come later, with help from Dr. Ruth.
3. "Sons" — a sexist word — is withdrawn out of respect for the U.S. feminist movement.

4. "Glowing eyes" have not been normally observed in Canada, outside radiology departments.
5. "The True North" was possibly provocative, till Canada has built an icebreaker big enough to convince the Americans that the Canadian Arctic extends farther than North Toronto.
6. More realistic than "From far and wide," a line that most Canadians cannot remember with a gun pointed at their heads.
7. "We stand on guard" implies an armed might that this country limits to Brinks (Canada) Ltd.
8. "Keep" was an unfortunate reminder that, militarily, Canada is a kept nation.
9. "Glorious and free" — the phrase was removed as too dependent on Wayne Gretzky's staying in Canada.
10. A simple yet eloquent expression of our enlightened self-interest.

Canadian independence — does it have a prayer?

The Ten Can-Commandments
For Canadians who want to stay that way even unto Eternity, the ten commandments are:

1. Thou shalt not make unto thee any graven image, except it hath the Queen's head on one side and a whole beaver on the other.
2. Thou shalt not take the name of the Lord in vain, but shalt remember what comes after "God save our gracious Queen . . ."

3. Remember the sabbath day, by shopping in Canada.
4. Six days shalt thou labour, unless told otherwise by a wholly independent Canadian labour union.

What price Old Glory?

5. Honour thy father and thy mother, that thy days may be long in the house after thou hast failed to make it in the States.
6. Thou shalt not kill. Canada is underpopulated as it is.
7. Thou shalt not commit adultery, by sleeping with thy U.S. Cabbage Patch doll.
8. Thou shalt not steal, or have income from American investments.
9. Thou shalt not covet thy neighbour's house, thou shalt not covet thy neighbour's swimming pool, nor his lower unemployment rate, nor his Declaration of Independence, nor his large pepperoni pizza.
10. Thou shalt not believe that there is a good reason why Canadians are taken for granted, dull, wimperialist, and possessing the spirit of wallpaper paste.

Response

Let us pray. O Lord, lead us Canadians not into the temptation of selling our birthright for a mess of potage, though it be Campbell's Chunky Potage.

Let us sing "God Bless America" only upon the crossing of our fingers.

What is a nation profited, if we shall gain the whole world, and lose our own soul, plus sales tax?

Give unto us the power to love one another, as doth the American people, or at least to send a postcard.

If the meek shall inherit the earth, let us glory in the Meeker that is Howie!

For, truly, blah is beautiful.

So shalt the choice for Canadians be this: To go to Hell in the comfort of thy neighbour's limo, or be proud and independent enough to make the descent in a handbasket of genuine Inuit design.

For truly the lion and the lamb shall lie down together, but do the twain getteth up?

American medical costs are very high; one should be sick before seeing a doctor

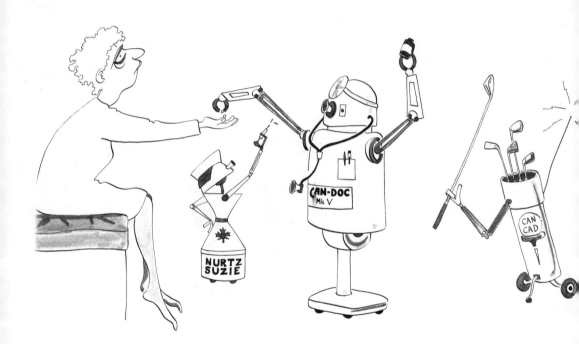

Medicare pays most expenses in Canada; however, a good many medical people have packed up and gone to the States

Epilogue
A Fun Exercise!

You have reached the end of the book. Congratulations! Maybe you skipped a few pages, but who's counting? The main question is: Has the material in this book made you feel:

    (1) proud to be a Canadian?
    (2) ready to be assimilated by the U.S.A.?
    (3) just vaguely nauseated?

By the time this book appears in the bookstores, the U.S.-Canada trade talks may have been aborted because:

    (1) The negotiators came down with shingles. And shakes.
    (2) The game was called on account of acid rain.
    (3) The Canadians became suspicious when a CIA agent was caught on the roof of the House of Commons, practising running the Stars and Stripes up the flagpole.

Assuming that the talks are still on, however, and if free trade with the U.S. means greater prosperity for

Canada though yours is one of the jobs made redundant by cheaper American imports, and you are fired, will you:

  (1) Frame your pink slip and hang it over the fireplace?
  (2) Be gloriously happy that other Canadians are better off?
  (3) Start chasing cars with American licence plates, trying to bite the tires?

Knowing that all that the Americans really need from Canada is our water, how do you feel about:

  (1) bathing in sand?
  (2) being able to afford whiskey but not the chaser?
  (3) going down a playland flume that debouches in Dallas?

The Americans want everything on the table, except our feet. Which would *you* sooner have:

  (1) Cheaper American cars, or a Canada that includes Ontario?
  (2) More jobs in Canada for carvers of souvenir totem poles, or our shirt?
  (3) Promotion to primary target for Soviet nukes, or having to pay more for coffin handles?

Canadian nationalists fear that the American free-traders are trying to make Canada sell its soul to the

States. How much do you estimate our soul to be worth ($U.S.):

    (1) One trillion?
    (2) One billion?
    (3) One million?
    (4) A Scout knife with genuine Rocky Mountain staghorn handle?

If you believe that Canada's economic and political independence is not for sale at any price, what is the best way to let our federal government know your strong sentiments:

    (1) Drop the prime minister a postcard?
    (2) Ask Opposition Leader John Turner to marry you?
    (3) Hold your breath till you turn red, white, and blue?

As a nation, Canada is in much the same state of cohesion as England when that country was waiting for the Angles, Jutes, and Saxons to fuse into a nation. (Think of Brian Mulroney as Ethelred the Unsteady.) The Angles, Jutes, and Saxons might have remained strictly multicultural had they not been firmly united by fury at the Normans for trying to make them eat with a fork.

Canada's Normans (Quebec) may yet produce a similar happy breed, given time to develop more cutlery. Indicate how long Canada should wait before signing any free-trade agreement that might compromise our nationhood:

(1) Five years.
(2) One hundred years.
(3) Till we see a rock video of the Fathers of Con-
    federation singing "Born in the U.S.A."

Eric Nicol and Dave More are two Canadian achievers who have never even tried to make it in the States.

Eric Nicol, despite his M.A. in French, has been making people laugh with his writings for more than thirty years. A three-time winner of the Leacock Medal for Humour, he has dozens of published books to his credit and also writes for radio, television, the stage, newspapers, and magazines. He lives in Vancouver, which may help explain his political outlook: anarchist in theory, liberal in practice, Canadian by birth and by choice.

Dave More is a graduate of the Alberta College of Art, where he subsequently instructed in design, painting, and drawing. He has also worked as an art history researcher and a medical graphics artist, but since 1978 has devoted his full energies to painting and satirical cartooning. More's paintings are represented in private and corporate collections across Canada, including the major energy companies, the Canadian Art Bank, and the Alberta Art Foundation. More and his wife, photographer Yvette Brideau, now pursue their respective art forms in Red Deer, Alberta.

Nicol and More have previously collaborated on four books for Hurtig Publishers, including *The Joy of Hockey, Golf/The Agony & the Ecstasy,* and *Tennis/ It Serves You Right!*

Photo montage by Yvette Brideau and Dave More
Eric Nicol's curate hat courtesy his father
Dave More's bowler hat courtesy Wilma B.
Moose courtesy Red Deer Museum and Archives